Chazisims

Conversations Between Me and My Kid.

Sherriece (Big Reese) Jones

Table of Contents

Dedication

This book is dedicated to my daughter Chaz Abrie Kidd. You are the love and strength of my life. You give me hope and inspire me to always do my best and more. May we always continue to have these crazy conversations I value so much. I hope they are as real as my love is for you. Love you sweetness now and forever.

Introduction

In a forever-changing world, our children need to be expressive and not hushed by a traditional silence passed down from generation to generation. Children should be seen and not heard does not apply in my home. I believe that is part of the problem. How do we know what and how they feel if we don't let them express themselves?   As long as it is respectful and it makes sense or even if it doesn't at the time it is essential for self-development as well as social skills. Chatter on children!!

The Pound Cake Caper

So, Chaz absolutely loves pound cake. I brought one Friday night and gave her a thick slice. Last night she asked for another piece so I went to open the box and it had deep holes and all kinds of pinches in the cake!

Me: Chaz did you do this?

Chaz: No mom why would I do that? I think it was a mouse!

Now unfortunately we do sometimes have field mice so I immediately started checking the other snacks but no hole or chew marks.

Me: Chaz you sure you didn't do this? (Of course, I knew she was lying) Well did you?

Chaz: Yes, I'm sure I didn't I promise.

Dad: Ress if she said she didn't do it then she didn't, let it go. (Such a daddy's girl)

So I say nothing else about it and give it the benefit of the doubt. I'm still checking for holes, droppings or anything that looks like the mouse could indeed be the culprit. So, later on that day I called Chaz and said ….

Me: Welp Chaz before I call the exterminator and pay 500.00 are you sure you didn't pinch off that cake? If you tell the truth I won't be mad, however I would not appreciate you lying to me but you would never get a spanking over food.

Chaz: Nope mom I mean if I tell the truth I won't get in trouble?

Finally, the break through so I thought then she said

Chaz: Nope mom I didn't.

Me: Ok Chaz.

As I'm walking out the door.

Chaz: Mom did you pay 500.00 for the exterminator yet?

Me: Not yet babe why?

Chaz: I'm sorry mommy I did it! I'm sorry I just love pound cake and I shouldn't have lied to you or on Mickey! I'm so sorry!

Me: No, you shouldn't have! Not only did you tell a lie I had to throw a perfectly good pound cake in the trash and nobody got any! You never have to lie, especially over food. Little girl don't make me not trust you or believe anything you say! If you lie about pound cake you will lie about anything! If you lie you will steal!

Dad: Chaz you did that?!

Me: Yeah sucka! I know my kids and I know when they're lying!

Chaz: Mommy I won't steal I promise. I'm sorry I lied! Mom where is the garbage bag?

Me: Why?

Chaz: That cake was still in the box! My mouth was watering when you tossed it. I was thinking if I could see If it's still there! So, you know we could get it out and finish it off!

Me: What!!

Chaz: just kidding, I'm really sorry I lied. I love you mommy!

Me: Love you too! Don't do that shit again! Lien will get your ass whooped!

Chaz: Ok mom.

Case solved!!

The Panties

Chaz: Ummm mom are those sheep or clouds on your panties?

Me: What? Sheep.

Chaz: Poor sheep.

Me: What? Don't start no shit Chaz! Cause I'm in the mood for ass breaking tonight!

Chaz: Well since you mentioned butt breaking you're a lot of women and those sheep might be struggling to count or just broke, crushed or just plain flattened!

Me: Well I'm not struggling to count! I'm giving you the count of 5 to get the hell outta my room!

Chaz: Ok but...can I take those poor dead smashed sheep with me?

Me: Get the hell outta here you demon spawn!

Chaz: Jesus take the wheel and the sheep!!

Booty Beans

Me: WTH! Why am I washing jelly beans!

Chaz: Oh shoot I took these from momma house and forgot they were in my back pocket! I was going to give you some.

Me: WTH I don't want no booty beans!

Chaz: (snatching air) Girl!! They are warm, chewy and gooey! Plus, I know how to wash so they are the cleanest booty beans you would have ever had!

Me: Yuck! I really don't like kids!!

Little Sister

Chaz: Hey Ress I want a little sister.

Me: (pulling the cover over my head) What!!?? Well, let me know when she gets here.

Chaz: Ms. Reese I'm over the stork stuff now I'm almost 9! So, stop playing and have that girl I'm getting lonely.

Me: Chaz please leave me alone! I'm not having nothen! Call your nephew if you're lonely!

Chaz: Nephew? I aint say northern about a nephew I said a sister! Omg forget it be selfish!

Me: Lord give me strength!

Chaz: Lord give me a sister!!

The Long Talk Good Night

Me: Good night my sweet little weasel!

Chaz: Is that Arizona watermelon juice chilling is a large mug filled with ice on your table my little lumpy love cake?

Me: Yes, my little pucky lipped possum.

Chaz: Well I'm quite parched and was wondering may I have a sip? You do know I don't pee the bed. My hot purple pancake.

Me: No mam my little two-toned tight chicken! Go get your own.

Chaz: I will...my stingy cruel mother who won't let the only little daughter she has die of thirst. I'll just ask daddy. Besides you had lemon pound cake and are known to have some serious backwash!

Me: I don't have no damn backwash Chaz! What the devil are you talking about!

Chaz: Now Ms Reese everybody has backwash! You didn't brush your teeth so dem crumbs are hanging around in your mouth and floating in that glass that is definitely backwash my little chocolate pie!

Me : Take your rusty ass to bed you little wood whesile !

Chaz: Wow no nice names huh? Mom no more cake for you oh and you got crumbs in your hair!

Parent Teacher Conference

Chaz: Good Morning Ms. Reese!

Me: Good Morning Greedy Weedy!

Chaz: Ummmm ummm got that student of the month. I've been bringing home A's and you haven't any bad dojo's…

Me: Chaz please you talk too much! Since kindergarten you have the same thing on every report card YOU TALK TOO MUCH!!

Chaz: So does that mean I'm in trouble?

Me: You tell me! Girl dont let me get to this school and it's more than you just talking too much!!

Chaz: In the case of 10-year-old Chaz she is not getting her Xbox taken! You wanna know why? Cause Ms. Reese you are not the momma!

Me: In the case of 10-year-old Chaz not only getting her Xbox taken, being on punishment and getting out of my face! It's because I am and will always be the momma!

Chaz: OMG!

Sneaker Game

Me: Hey Chaz you like Polo sneakers?

Chaz: Are they Polo associated?

Me: No Ralph Lauren..wait what do you know about something being associated??

Chz: Well Keyion said don't let mommy put that bs on your feet. He said if it's associated it's not Polo. You know like Vans for example they are manufactured in California it's a skateboard sneaker and they're real.

Me: Ok first of all I don't put bs on your feet!

Chaz: Ms. Reese ,Ms. Reese calm down the boy knows his sneakers. He was just making sure I got sauce and my sneaker game in on fleek!

Me: Keyion better shut the hell up and for that tell me what associated means.

Chaz: It means a connection with someone or a business or something like that.

Me: Smart ass.

Chaz: Exactly!

Me: Keep listening to Key. He will be buying you stuff.

Chaz: He won't let me suffer he will buy it.

Me: Get outta my face! Can't stand you or him! (Love my kids)

Let's Talk Hair

Chaz: Hey Ms. Reese what are you doing?

Me: Shaving.

Chaz: Why?

Me: So, I don't look like a wildebeest.

Chaz: Wildebeest? What's that?

Me: Something nasty and hairy looking if you don't shave. Hair hold odors.

She puts her head down.

Me: What's wrong baby?

Chaz: I was so excited I got 2 hairs under one arm and 4 under the other and I don't want to shave or cut them.

Me: You don't have too babe. Your way too young anyway.

Chaz: I know that's right! I'm proud of my hair I just would have to be a baby wildebeest cause I'm not shaving nothing!

Me: So, you gonna be a woman of the bush??

Chaz: What's that mom?

Me: Never you mind little girl, never you mind.

A Day Off

Me: So, you got a day off? No school tomorrow

Chaz: Oh, that's absolutely wonderful!

Me: Why? You are still getting on that computer.

Chaz: Omg this is not Village charter school this
______Pennington Ave!! So please Sweet Rees don't
make me work. Just let me squeeze you girl!

Me: I'm going to squeeze my foot in your behind little girl!
Chaz: I have a hard enough time. I don't need a foot, toe,
heel or nothing else for that matter. I don't even like Scott
but I gotta use him!

Me: Scott??? Oh girl smh get outta here!

Chaz: No problem just keep your feet on the ground.
Love you mommy!

Hell

Chaz: Hey Ms. Reese is "what the hell "a curse word ? If not can I say it?

Me: Yes it is a curse word and no you can't say it but you can say H.E double hockey sticks

She turns around and says to the dog.

Chaz: Zanzi what the H.E double hockey sticks you got going on? Over there snoring like a grown man!

Me: Jesus!

Inspiration

Chaz: Mom I wanna be an inspiration

Me: What does inspiration mean?

Chaz: Mommy you don't know that word?

Me: Yes, I just wanna make sure you do,

Chaz: inspirational, creative to inspire, flair!

Me: Ok who do you want to inspire?

Chaz: Girls my age. Tall, fat, short or skinny we are all beautiful and should never be ashamed of how we look and who we are.

Me: That's wonderful Chaz! I'm glad you're paying attention when I'm talking to you. I can't take all the credit though you have very strong women in your life.

Chaz: Do I have fast ones?

Me: Fast ones? I'm sure but why did you ask me that?

Chaz: Cause if you decide to really beat me one day I want to make sure I'm inherited speed so I can run!

Me: Please exit my room.

What's Really Going On?

Chaz: Hey Ms. Reese Im going to spend the night with Uncle David

Me: Ok hound cat go ahead then.

Chaz: Hold up you super siked up! What are you having a party? I think it's some partying when I'm not home! You be dropping it like it's hot! I knew it!! Go Ms. Reese!

Me: The only thing that's gonna drop like it's hot is this belt on your ass!

Chaz: Why is it I get threatened with a wack?

Me: Omg Chaz please hush!

Chaz: (mumbling under her breath) humph when you wanna talk especially about work I'll remember you want me to be quiet!

Stomach Pains

Chaz: Mom omg my stomach hurts and no I don't need to poop and no I don't want a ginger ale.

Me: So if you're telling me all that you don't need then what do you want me to do? I know what that baby needs, let mommy rub your back so you can burp.

Chaz: I don't need a back rub or a burp Ms. Reese!

Me: Chaz you are working my last nerve! What's wrong with you! Cause I'm telling you right now you're taking your hypochondriac ass to school!

Chaz: Ok you know what I want some empathy! I need a new night light, I need to watch full house until I go to sleep, I need you to crack my window cause I'm hot, I don't need Zanzabar on my bed with his super bad breath! I really just need your bed mommy.

Me: Aww baby (I hug her) you know what you need?

Chaz: What my beautiful, wonderful mom who's gonna let me sleep with her.

Me: I need you to stop playing with me, I need you to go to bed and if you don't you're going to need Jesus! Now Good Night!

Chaz: Oh, I see well good night and God Bless.

(2 hours later I go in her room)

Me: Baby you ok?

Chaz: Instant mommy karma! You can't sleep either. Come on Ms. Reese lets go to bed.

Income Tax Check

Chaz: Hey Ms Reese what are you doing?

Me: What you should be doing brushing your teeth!

Chaz: Brush extra hard you were smoking hookah last night!

Me: Wait what! Hush your mouth I need to finish your school shopping so I can get it out the way.

Chaz: Mom really! You did all my summer shopping, all my shopping for the winter now all my school shopping!? There goes all your tax money smh!

Me: What you know about some income tax money! You don't work in anybody's pie factory so what do you know about taxes?

Chaz: My friend told me her mom said her step dad ain't getting none of her income tax check and he's not claiming them this year cause she got a job! There having McDonalds tonight! She said she's gonna buy all their clothes and her brother DayDay can have his pizza party now. I told her at least I did get clothes but I haven't seen any McDonalds yet.

Me: You're not either! Chaz go brush your teeth talking about some damn DayDay!

The Sneaker Con.

Chaz: Can I have a pair of white sneakers?

Me: Yes, Chaz what kind?

Chaz: Well, I would like a pair of Stephen Currys.

Me: What are those?

Chaz: Mom He's a basketball player.

Me: Girl you know, I know nothing about sports! You can have them though.

Chaz: Mom I passed the 5th grade.

Me: I'm aware of that Chaz.

Chaz: I was thinking I need those black Jordan's oh and those gray ones too! Dad bought me shirts. I can match them with the sneakers if you don't mind.

Me: Oh, hell no!! I do mind! I'm not made of money, go ask your dad.

Chaz: He said the same thing. Please I wont ask for another thing until my birthday I promise!

Me: You know what! If I buy these sneakers you're not getting nothin' else!!

Chaz: I understand mom, you're the best mom ever! I love you now, come here sweet thang and let me rub your feet.

Me: Get your little begging ass out of here smh!

We Are Talking Berries.

Chaz: Mommy you look extra black

Me: What?? I am black and black is beautiful.

Chaz: Well ok so you're extra beautiful too.

Me: Thanks, Chazzy humph! The blacker the berry the sweeter the juice the yellower the bitter.

Chaz: Mom that's not really your color so when it disappears are you gonna be bitter?

Me: Chaz just go eat your lunch smh!

Breakfast.

Chaz: I'm hungry mom.

Me: Hi Chaz I'm Reese nice to meet you! You better go eat some cereal.

Chaz: I don't do cereal.

Me: Since when?? Girl you better take you tail downstairs and get that cereal!

Chaz: (hands on her hips) mom I'll see you downstairs and don't put cheese in the eggs. I don't do well with dairy in the morning. I don't want it messing with my stomach. Especially knowing I gotta go to school! You know you can't take a poop in peace there.

Me: Wth! Jesus!

Restless No Sleep.

Chaz: Mommmmmmmy

Me: What girl!!

Chaz: It's only 9:00 and you're already yelling. Did you sleep well?

Me: Abrie (middle name) I'm not in a good mood. Please help me get these clothes together for the wash.

Chaz: I'm in a good mood. You see all these kids I got? (Her dolls) I'm not stressed so relax and stop yelling. I mean I know I'm a lot sometimes. Just know I'm here for you. I love you mom.

Me: Your right moomp noomp Im just drained.I love you and I'm sorry for being grumpy.

Chaz: You sure about that?

Me: Yes, babe why?

Chaz: Cause the way you were snoring last night I thought you were in the bed fighting a bear!. I was scared for you!

Me: Chaz get the hell outta my face before I slap you! Smh!!

Rolling Thunder.

Chaz: Can I watch you cook?

Me: Chaz baby it's late. Go take a bath so you can get ready for camp.

Chaz: Can I skip a bath tonight?

Me: Umm no sister girl we skip no bathes or showers in this house. Go wash that camp off! Smelling like sweet dirt and a musty billy goat!

Chaz: Wait a minute now! I might smell like dirt, camp and cookies but I sure don't smell like nobody's goat!

Me: I said you do.

Chaz: I said I don't! That must mean daddy is a mule and you're a donkey because that's the animal's you say I smell like when you think I stink which I don't! I smell like vanilla bean spray!

Me: The only beans you smell like is pork and beans! Now go wash!

Chaz: Is this a farm or a supermarket? Telling me I smell like all these animals and food! Whatever happened to the hoagie shop!

Get In Your Own Bed!

Dad: Chaz you are sleeping in your own bed tonight.

Chaz: Why daddy?

Dad: Cause sometimes daddy and mommy need some alone time.

Chaz: Oh yeah?

(I walk in the room)

Chaz: Mom what kind of alone time you and dad need? What's going on here?

Me: What are you talking about girl?

Chaz: Well dad said y'all need some alone time and I don't appreciate that! When you had me there was no more alone time! So what time are you coming to get me outta my bed? I don't have all night!

Me: YOU BETTER TAKE YOUR ALMOST! 11-YEAR-OLD ASS AND GET IN YOUR OWN BED!! YOU ARE A MESS!! YOUR TIME IS OVER!!

Chaz: NEVER!! I'm going to sleep with yall til Im 35 cause that's when dad said I can have a boyfriend! So, until then it's US time.

Me: Good night Chaz.

Dad: Reese are you serious??

Me: You hush your lips! Nobody told you to tell her she couldn't have a boyfriend til she was 35.

Charlot

Chaz: Mommy, Mommy!! There's a spider in my room!!

Me: Kill it then! Stop screaming like a wild cheetah!

Chaz: Jesus mom! I tell you there's a spider in my room
and you won't come kill it! Then you call me a wild
cheetah on top of that! I don't want any Charlottes in my
room! (reference From Charlotte's Web)

Me: Well as junkie as your room is you might as well
have Charlotte's cause you're a Wilbur and don't call the
Lord's name out in vain!

Chaz: I might as well he's the only one who is gonna
save me. You haven't made a move yet!

Me: If you don't get the hell outta my room your gonna
need him! Keep talking junk!

Chaz: I guess because at the rate you're moving it will lay
eggs like the movie and then they will be everywhere!
Just call an exterminator smh!

Phone Photos.

Chaz: Ms. Reese!! What in the cotton-picking world! Who are you laying on?

Me: Toot what are you talking about?

Chaz: This ain't my daddy!

Me: What are you talking about girl! Let me see.

Chaz: Covering up evidence is gonna help Im telling!

(I snatch my phone)

Me: Girl that's your dad you see his ring and finger nails. Besides if you ever tell anything on me I will twist your lips!

Chaz: Ummm I couldn't see your head looks super big in this picture so don't be aggressive. If you twist my lips dad will untwist them and ask how they got that way. You want that kind of trouble?

Me: Chaz omg!

Chaz: It will be one of those unfortunate situations we talked about.

Me: WTH!! Chaz hush lol!!

Beauty and the Beast

Me: Why did Bell decide to take her nosy ass in the west wing! Didn't that ugly furry sapsucka tell her not too!

Chaz: Mom are you serious? He made her run away after she was willing to look at his ugly face and lord only knows how his breath and body smells! He got some nerve hollering at her. He only took one bath through the whole movie! Filthy self with those one pair of pants!

Me: Well she still is nosy!

Chaz: She went and put on that yellow dress and forgot all about it. Come to think of it you need a yellow dress.

Me: For what?

Chaz: For when you make dad mad he will forget all about it.

Me: Nope yellow is not my color.

Chaz: Well Johnny Gill said you can put on a red one.

Me: What?? LOL!!!

Beets....

Me: Hey mom you got more beets?

Mom:Yeah there in the refrigarator .

Me: I'm gonna get some before I go.

Chaz: Mom what's that?

Me: Beets wanna try one (She eats one)

Chaz: What in the sam …

Me: You better not!

Chaz: That mess tastes like dirt and ketchup! I best stop begging!

Me: You think?

Chaz: I wasn't thinking because if I was I wouldn't have asked. Being greedy is hard work. I think I'm going to retire today.

Mom: Where the hell did you get her from?! Wait don't answer, just take her back!

What's for Dinner?

Chaz: What for dinner today Ms. Reese today?

Me: What, you're greedy but didn't even eat breakfast or lunch and you're asking about dinner?

Chaz: (standing there looking crazy) uhhh yeah I have to see what I'll have room for after I eat lunch at school then lunch here it's a half a day.

Me: I don't know what your stomach has room for but I know what my foot has room for if you don't play like Mike and beat it.

Chaz: Now why.. Just why would you do that? After breakfast I eat not 1 but 2 lunches so I'll need my but to make room for dinner with a fresh roll of toilet paper. I'm low.

Me: Cause you eat too much!

Chaz: Unbelievable! First I eat too much food and now I use too much toilet paper. Can't eat, cant poop, can't play my game so what can I do!?

Me: Go catch your bus.

Chaz: Now that's something I wish I didn't have to do!
Have a great day mommy.

Me: You too love you!

Chaz: Ummmm Hmmmmm

Key's Birthday Wish.

Chaz: Mom I love Keyion!

Me: Me too baby.

Chaz:I Heard what Keyion wants for his birthday.

Me: What?

Chaz: He said he wants a midget!

Me: LOL!!!

Chaz: Why does he want a midget for? That's like being with a kid with a ginormous butt!

Me: The midgets he's talking about are adults.

Chaz: Well he better not bring one here cause we are going right upstairs to play in my kitchen.

Me: LOL smh!

I'm Starving!

Chaz: Hey Tony (Don't know why she calls me that) You slapping pots today?

Me: Girl can I take off my coat first? (She starts taking off my coat for me) Unhand me girl!

Chaz: Listen Tony I want some home cooked meal! Ummmm Hmmmm.Im starving. My lunch didn't hit on anything (pointing at her stomach) I need to get down on some grub bub! Some delicious delight! I've been dreaming about chow.

Me: Are you done! Little greedy self.

Chaz: Yes, I would like biscuits and put a lot of onions in that medium brown gravy. I don't like it too dark. I need to see them!

Me: Ok Chaz I'm going to feed you bricks and butter!!!

Chaz: Get one from the front and I will love it! Just add garlic to that butter cause the bricks already look well done!

Me: Are you serious?? Get outta here!

Sneaker Head.

Chaz: Hey Ms. Reese I need a new pair of Jordans, you know the ones with the lights.

Me: Oh yeah i just brought you a pair of all black ones. It's not my fault you stomp out forest fires with your shoes. take better care of them.

Chaz: Ms. Resse please I asked you before I asked Keyion. I know he will buy them.

Me: Well you got a better chance with him cause I just bought those Jordans, 2 pairs of keds and some converses. I still have to pay for your Christmas stuff too.

Chaz: So, I guess I need to get creative?? If we still got Christmas lights I can make it work!

Me: I can't with you!

Baby for Hire.

Chaz: Oh Lord nobody is hiring.

Me: What?

Chaz: I'm trying to get a job to help out. The struggle is real! Nobody wants to hire a 9-year-old. I was looking all night mom. Not even toys r us where a kid can be a kid!

Me: Girl the only job you need is to be 9. The only work you have to do is your school work I'll handle the rest ladybug.

Chaz: Well you let me know cause I will work.

Me: Smh lol thank you baby! I love you.

Thanksgiving.

Me: (Me and her dad are talking about Thanksgiving) I gotta rush home and cook for us and Coles house.

Chaz: Mom we having dinner here too?

Dad: Yeah Chaz we gotta have something to eat for us.

Chaz: What are you making for auntie Coles?

Me: Not sure.

Chaz: Oh well make sure you bring the rest home.

Dad: You don't do that Chaz. whatever you take to someone's home you leave it there.

Chaz: I don't know what's wrong with daddy! Cause ima tell you right now If I go to somebody's house If I bring juice and there's some left I'm taking it to drink on the way home! If I bring cake I'm taking it home to eat down to the crumbs. I might have a stomach ache after but I will be ok. Oh, don't let it be turkey left, I'll eat that and take the bones home for Zanzi!

Me: That's just greedy and you will do no such thing! You want people to think you have any manners? You know better.

Chaz: Mommy you look hungry right now I guess I'll save you some too. You're the one always talking about is everyone good? Do you want anything else! Shoot I'm going hungry and coming back extra full then I'll be good and won't want anything else!

Me: Jesus (She cuts me off)

Chaz: As for our house I'll start the blessing of the food on the ride home so we can eat soon as we hit the door.

Me: Chaz!!

Sick in Bed.

Me: Chaz I called the doctor you can't get an appointment until December, but they did tell me what to do.

Chaz: I don't know why you called the doctor. The only doctor I'm going to see is Mcstuffins. She comes on at 11:30.

Me: Girl!! You might need to take your rusty but to the hospital sounding like a truck.

Chaz: Oh well give me some oil. They are not about to be picking and poking at me while I'm sitting in that paper robe that tears and all my booty be out! Plus, I be freezing. They don't even offer a sister a blanket and let's not even go into having a flu shot. I've seen people walking backwards on YouTube from taking that.

Me: You watch too much YouTube! Chazzy bean what am I going to do with you?

Chaz: How bout some hot tea and soup for starters?

Me: You got it!

No Leftovers.

Chaz: Ms.Reese What's for dinner?

Me: Nothing, I'm not cooking.

Chaz: Why?

Me: I cooked for Thanksgiving and I'm not cooking anymore until tomorrow.

Chaz: What in the devil! That was Thursday! I'm tired of greens, beans, tomatoes, potatoes, ram, lamb, chicken and turkey! You name it and I don't want it!!

Me: Well cook something then.

(She goes to the freezer)

Chaz: Well It's some ground turkey in here. I guess I can do hamburger helper its rough round here after the holidays.

Me: LOL!!!!

Bugs for Christmas.

Me: Chaz I'm about to go get the tree for Christmas.

Chaz: Yayyy Mommy I can't wait!!!

(Chaz is terrified of any bugs. 2 Spiders come out the tree)

Chaz: Mommy!!!!!!! Mommy!!!! Its spiders in the tree!!!!! Kill them!!!! Kill them dead!!!! OMG!!!!

Me: Wait a damn minute Chaz!! Stop all that damn yelling! (I stomp the poor spiders to death) Your big mouth gave me a headache!

Chaz: You know I'm scared just cause I had spinach it didn't give me courage!

Me: Wth are you talking about?? Now come on an help me

(This girl is standing at the top of the steps with tears in her eyes)

Chaz: No mommy that tree got spiders, snakes, flies and bees, beetles, bed bugs, cats and fleas that's why I don't do fake trees! You name it!!! You name it!!

Me: And you made it rhyme lol!!!!

V Bucks.

Chaz: Mom dad said he was going to buy me some V Bucks.

Me: And I'm going to punch him! Those people make billions off our poor black asses!

Chaz: It's no different than buying weave, wigs and lashes there getting rich off of poor people too.

Me: Silent___________ummmm well.

Chaz: SMH so can we still want V Bucks for Fort knight and yall can still want weave from the hair store. Problem solved!

Me: Ok Chaz.

Paranormal

Me: Chaz why the hell are all these sunflower seeds in this carpet! I just stepped on one!

Chaz: Mom you won't believe it I think something is really in here!

Me: Huh?

Chaz: The other day I was sitting here playing my game and my water started moving! I was like what the heck! I was too scared to move!

Me: Oh Yeah well where was I? Why didn't you call me? Furthermore, what does that have to do with sunflower seeds!

Chaz: I'm getting to that mom. So, what I think happened is the ghost got hungry and just ate all the seeds and just spit them anywhere! So disrespectful! Maybe he just needs a friend like Casper!

Me: Oh Yeah well he's gonna get his wish! If you don't get your natural born black but off that bed and clean up these seeds it's going to be an extra ghost in this house!

Ghost my ass! The stuff you come up with doesn't make any sense!

Chaz: Ok I'm trying to tell he's deep he even ate your reese pieces and drank that last ginger ale!

Me: Well I got a belt that whoops the dead! If YOU ate my candy and drank my soda im going to Kick, Chop and tiger roll both yall asses!

Chaz: Well Clyde the gig is up!

Me: Who is Clyde?

Chaz: The ghost!

Me: Chaz!! Clean up these seeds and get Clyde to help you!! Oh yeah while you're at it cough up my candy and soda!

Young Queen

Chaz: I am a Young Queen from a line of strong black women. My mom is raising me to be strong, well spoken, caring and compassionate. I will continue my education and be a force to be reckoned with. My life is mine and my soul belongs to my father and savior. Love is the light I want to follow.

Me: Well said ...well said!